Ethereum
Programming, mining,
pool investment 2018

facts, and as such any inattention, use or misuse of the information in question by the reader will render any resulting actions solely under their purview. There are no scenarios in which the publisher or the original author of this work can be in any fashion deemed liable for any hardship or damages that may befall them after undertaking information described herein.

Additionally, the information found on the following pages is intended for informational purposes only and should thus be considered, universal. As befitting its nature, the information presented is without assurance regarding its continued validity or interim quality. Trademarks that mentioned are done without written consent and can in no way be considered an endorsement from the trademark holder.

Introduction

Ethereum is a decentralized platform. Decentralized means merely that there is no single authority in charge; power is dispersed among all the users. This means it's harder to hack, because there is no single weak point, and there's zero downtime, which means the platform never shuts down.

The Ethereum blockchain's focus is on running the codes necessary for programming any decentralized application. We notice that it is different from the bitcoin blockchain that can be used to keep track of the ownership of digital currency. Bitcoin only offers a peer-to-peer electronic cash system that makes online Bitcoin payments possible. But in the Ethereum blockchain, miners do not mine for bitcoins; rather they work to earn "Ether," which is a crypto token that powers the network. It goes one step beyond a cryptocurrency that can only be used to trade by also being used by application developers to pay for the transaction fees incurred and other services in the Ethereum network.

The buzz of Bitcoin is still ringing in many investors ears, and they are looking for the next cryptocurrency windfall. Some hope that Ethereum just might be what they are looking for. In addition to this, there are also many who are simply interested in the implications mentioned above of the blockchain itself. These Ethereum participants wish to be a part of the revolution that they foresee taking place.

But either way, you look out it, Ethereum is indeed, one-part cryptocurrency and one-part technological innovation. For this book, we will take a two-pronged approach and inundate ourselves with each one of these ingredients that make up what is "Ethereum."

Whether you plan to invest in Ether as a currency simply or you want to build a revolutionary application on the Ethereum platform, it is critical to understand the role of both the currency and the larger framework. In the cryptocurrency space, as of today, Ether is second only to Bitcoin regarding popularity and value. In a few short years, it has gained considerable traction and become a forerunner in the burgeoning blockchain revolution.

Throughout this book, we will examine Ethereum's distinct approach to blockchain technology as a technological framework for building decentralized applications. We will cover what this means, how these applications work, and what you need to know if you're thinking about investing in Ether, a project built on the Ethereum platform, or even developing your Ethereum-based application.

Chapter 1: History of Ethereum

Origin of the name "Ethereum."

The founder of Ethereum, Buterin had come across the term Ethereum when he was glancing through a list of elements listed in science fiction. Vitalik liked the word Ether and the meaning associated with it. Ether means air, and it also represents a medium that is permeable to light. If you were interested in playing WoW, then you would have perhaps wondered if he got the idea of the name "Ethereum" from the ethereal race in the game that resides in Netherstorm. Any link from this game to Ethereum is purely incidental and nothing more than it.

The Ethereum platform has been in existence for a couple of years but has just recently begun the forward march to success, going into partnership with Microsoft to release software, present the BaaS toolkit and so much more besides. It is more often referred to as the "brainchild" of Vitalik Buterin, a Russian-Canadian prodigy regarding computer programming. When he was just 19 years old, he was a real enthusiast of sociology, politics, economics, epistemology, cryptology and information theory and, in 2013, he released the first white paper on his idea.

Around the same time, Vitalik began to work with Dr. Gavin Wood, and they then co-founded the Ethereum Foundation, a legal entity that manages both the legal and marketing efforts of Ethereum. In April 2014, Gavin published the Ethereum Yellow Paper that provided the technical specifications for the Ethereum Virtual Machine (EVM).

Following the detailed specifications in the Yellow Paper, today, Ethereum clients have been implemented in seven programming languages, namely C++, Go, Python, Java, JavaScript, Haskell, and Rust. In a bid to kick-start a community of developers, miners, and Ethereum investors, the Ethereum Foundation conducted a presale of more than 60 million Ethers (digital tokens).

Within the Bitcoin community, he couldn't find support, so he decided to try creating a new platform with a language that would allow it to be used for a variety of things, and not just a currency like Bitcoin. In the summer of 2014, Buterin ran a crowdsale to get funding, and Ethereum went live in July 2015. It gave out 11.9 million Ethers to those who participated in the crowdsale.

By 2014, Ethereum had established a core team of developers, gained considerable support, and was officially under development. A crowd-sale of the initial round of Ether, the digital currency used by Ethereum, took place in July-August of 2014, with proceeds funding further development of the software.

On July 30, 2015, the first iteration of Ethereum officially went live. Today, Ethereum is still maintained by a central team of developers, including founder Vitalik Buterin, and is managed by a Swiss non-profit organization called the Ethereum Foundation. Unlike Bitcoin, whose creator remains a mystery, Buterin serves as a figurehead for this project and his identity is very much tied to Ethereum. While many other programmers and thinkers are contributing to the development of Ethereum, Buterin is viewed as the inventor and the "face" of the project. Some critics have expressed concern over the centrality of the Ethereum project and a "cult of personality" surrounding Buterin.

Several prototypes of the Ethereum platform were developed by the Ethereum Foundation, as part of their Proof-of-Concept series, before the official launch of the Frontier network. The last of these prototypes culminated in a public beta pre-release known as "Olympic." The

Olympic network provided users with a bug bounty of 25,000 units of ether for stress testing the limits of the Ethereum blockchain.

One of the first major projects built on the Ethereum network was a venture capital fund referred to as "The DAO." We already introduced the concept of a Decentralized Autonomous Organization, so the name of this project should be both familiar and confusing. There can be any number of DAOs, but in this case we are referring to a specific organization, which simply called itself The DAO.

The DAO comprised the largest bundle of smart contracts on Ethereum and was the earliest, most publicized project on the platform. Its purpose was to collect money from investors and distribute it to projects that the investors voted on... similar to a venture capital firm. The DAO's operation was contained entirely on the Ethereum blockchain. It did not have a street address. It didn't have a Board of Directors. It was not incorporated under the laws of any nation or government. The DAO was just a set of rules and procedures codified in contracts stored in the blockchain. The DAO was so large, in fact, that it was able to raise roughly 170 million dollars in Ethereum tokens from investors.

Relation between Ethereum and banks

Taking into consideration the nature of banking industry and also the high level of security that banks will need for protecting their interest as well as their customer's interest, it can be said that Ethereum can be helpful for banks. The value of Ethereum will keep on increasing as banks start moving towards applications based on blockchain technology that uses Smart Contracts for automating the financial process. As the demand for Smart Contracts will increase, the value of Ethereum will increase as well. At present, there are about 11 major banks like Barclays, UBS, HSBC, and many more. These banks have got together with R3 (a startup and an innovation firm that aims at uplifting the role of technology in routine operations) for testing a system. This system will help banks in making use of blockchain for the sake of trading. This test is crucial because it makes use of the blockchain technology that is developed by Ethereum for enabling a Microsoft platform to run on it. If this test turns out to be a success, then not only will it mean that Ethereum will be incorporated into the banking system of these banks, but also revolutionize the entire banking system.

Chapter 2: Benefits of Ethereum

Ethereum Virtual Machine

Blockchain technology is revolutionary; however, before Ethereum, blockchains had limited capabilities and were mainly used for recording transactions.

One of the important innovations that Ethereum offered over existing blockchain technology was the Ethereum

Virtual Machine (EVM).

The Ethereum Virtual Machine allowed developers to create applications in computer programming languages similar to languages they are familiar with. These applications can be as advanced as any applications they could create on other computer platforms. They are run on the Ethereum Virtual Machine, which allows these decentralized applications to use blockchain technology with greater ease and lower costs than previously possible.

Decentralization

We may think we control our Facebook photos, computer files in cloud storage, or the messages in our chat application. However, these are controlled by centralized systems and companies.

When you upload photos to Facebook, all your images are stored on a central server owned by Facebook. This is the same for files you upload to Google Drive or other cloud storage.

When you send a message using a chat application, the message is sent to the central servers of the company, which then sends it from the server to the message recipient. The servers keep a record of all the messages. When you access your chat history, you access it from those servers.

Ethereum allows for the decentralization of applications and data, meaning there is no central server or company that controls all your data. Decentralized applications are run across a network of computers; if one computer goes offline, the data can be accessed from the other computers also running the application.

Many applications and websites we are familiar with today are being developed as decentralized versions on the Ethereum network. This includes decentralized cloud storage, messaging applications, social networks and more.

No Censorship

The decentralized structure of the Ethereum network means governments and companies can't censor websites and applications.

If a government wanted to censor a website, they could block access to the website or close the server running the website. If they wanted to censor a decentralized application, they would have to shut down every computer or server running that application.

The computers running dApps are spread across the entire world, making it impossible for one government to shut them all down.

With a decentralized network and applications, companies and governments can't censor content, ban applications, or obtain user data. This provides greater freedom of speech and puts control back in the hands of the users of applications running on Ethereum.

Users that post content that mentions Tibet, the Tiananmen Square massacre, or anything critical of the Chinese government will have that content removed in China. They may also be investigated by the Chinese government after posting it. Companies operating in China must ban content the government doesn't approve of and provide user data to the government.

11

If a user posts an image on Twitter, Facebook, or Instagram that the company doesn't approve of, they can remove the image and ban the user. This may not seem like a problem for most people, as they aren't posting anything against the rules of these companies. However, these companies must obey the laws of the countries they operate. Most social media platforms are banned in China, as foreign companies don't comply with the harsh censorship of the Chinese governments.

Ease of development

Designing a blockchain network is expensive, time-consuming, and complex, as it needs many people to provide computing power to a new blockchain network.

Developing applications that run on the Ethereum blockchain and EVM is relatively easy. The programming language is related to commonly used programming languages, such as JavaScript. As the programming language is similar to existing programming languages, developers can create programs easily with minimal additional learning.

Developers must create a new blockchain and build a network of computers and users that would support it.

Ethereum enables developers to use the existing Ethereum blockchain and network of computers. The Ethereum Virtual Machine also permits developers to build applications on blockchain technology, without needing to create their blockchain network.

Security

Numerous risks associated with existing centralized systems are significantly reduced with decentralized systems.

Decentralized servers are not as vulnerable to hacking or server failure. To hack a decentralized system, the hacker would need to control the majority of the computing power on the network. As the Ethereum network is hundreds of thousands of computers all over the world, it is almost impossible for someone to control the majority of the network.

Facebook, PayPal, banks, and most other companies have centralized servers. If those servers are hacked, then hackers may obtain all your data stored on those servers. If the central servers crash or go offline, then all the data is inaccessible.

Smart Contracts

Smart contracts are contracts written in computer code; they can execute automatically if the terms of a contract are met. There are no lawyers or courts required to enforce the terms of a contract.

While Bitcoin allowed payments across a blockchain, these payments were manual, such as selecting to send money to another person. Ethereum has allowed automatic payments that can be triggered when an event, milestone, or condition occurs.

Ethereum allows companies to develop applications and sell tokens or coins that can be used in the applications. These applications run on the Ethereum platform, and if an app becomes popular, the tokens used in the application should theoretically increase in value.

Companies can raise funds for their projects, without requiring loans or venture capital funding. Initial supporters of an application can also profit if the app becomes popular.

Ethereum has created a platform where decentralized apps (dapps) could run with smart contracts to replace this process. Instead of the Uber app, you could use a dApp that automatically executes smart contracts based on the distance traveled. This would work similar to the Uber example above, but it would operate on the Ethereum platform using Ether or an Ethereum token as payment.

This is one potential application of dApps and smart contracts. There are thousands of dApps in development that could change a wide range of industries.

New methods for funding companies and projects

Ethereum has opened new possibilities for companies and developers to raise money to fund their growth. While Initial Coin Offerings were possible before Ethereum, these were linked to the popularity of a new cryptocurrency.

Giant World Supercomputer

One of the most impressive advantages of Ethereum is that all the individual computers connected act like one giant worldwide supercomputer.

The computing power on the Ethereum network can be directed towards the Ethereum Virtual Machine. This allows applications to run, utilizing the power of one of the most powerful supercomputers in the world.

While the Bitcoin network is also connected like a worldwide supercomputer, the computing power of the Bitcoin network is directed towards processing transactions.

Chapter 3: Risks and Disadvantages of Ethereum

Ether is not designed for real-world transactions

Bitcoin and many other cryptocurrencies are more practical forms of payment with many accepted at shops and websites around the world. Using Ether will depend on the popularity of the Ethereum platform and the number of people running dApps and smart contracts.

Ether, the cryptocurrency used for payments on the Ethereum network, is used to pay for computing power to run dApps and smart contracts. Ether is not designed to be used for payments at shops, online, or as an alternative to other real-world payment methods.

Ether May Not Increase in Value

Even if developers and companies use the Ethereum platform, the price of Ether may not increase if there is a greater supply of Ether created or demand from traders decreases.

Even if the Ethereum platform gains in popularity, there is no guarantee the price of

Ether will increase. Many people buying Ether are purchasing it for speculative profit and do not intend to use it for running dApps or smart contracts.

Traders and speculators may overvalue the current price of Ether. If they sell, this may dramatically decrease the price of Ether.

New and Unproven Technology

Many dangers and risks involved with using Ethereum may still be unknown and may not become apparent until Ethereum is being used on a larger scale.

While many companies have joined an alliance to develop the use of Ethereum within their organizations, this is still at the research and feasibility stage. There have been few companies implementing Ethereum as a replacement for existing systems. There have also been a few mainstream dApps that have become popular.

Issues with Smart Contracts

A badly written smart contract allowed a group of people to exploit the contract and steal more than 50 million dollars.

Thousands of people looked at the code in the DAO smart contract, and most saw no issues.

The problems with the smart contract were only realized after they had been exploited.

With a standard legal contract, if there is poorly written wording that allows someone to exploit the contract, this can be taken to court. The disagreement over the wording and intention of a contract can be settled through legal proceedings.

Dangers of a Giant Worldwide Supercomputer

The Ethereum network and smart contracts have been compared to Skynet. Ethereum is a worldwide network of computers that are connected, running applications and code that can't be argued with.

In the DAO hack, people exploited a vulnerability in the code of a smart contract to steal more than 50 million dollars. While there are financial risks with smart contracts, there are also much greater security risks.

If there was an error in the code or the code was badly written, it opens the possibility that the smart contract doesn't run as intended. The contract could then run without being stopped or altered, leading to potentially disastrous consequences, especially if connected to government or military systems.

Hype around dApps

dApps offer many benefits over existing applications. However, throughout history, there have been many technologies with benefits over existing options but failed to gain mainstream adoption.

Convincing people to pay for a new application that is similar to a more popular free application they use may be difficult. Privacy and the benefits of decentralization may not be compelling enough reasons for people to use dApps over existing applications, especially if it will cost them money to use them.

Applications, such as Instagram and Facebook, are free; however, they use your personal information to allow advertisers to sell products and services to you. They are free for you to use, but your data is the product these companies are selling to other people.

dApps are controlled by the users, not by a centralized company. The users control their privacy and data. In exchange for this control, using the dApp will cost money. Uploading a photo, like a photo, and other actions on a photo sharing dApp may cost a certain amount of money for each action.

Chapter 4: Understanding Blockchain Technologies

Before we begin to dig into the specifics of Ethereum, it is crucial to understand some of the core principles of blockchain technology, in general. For newcomers to the cryptocurrency space, one of the concepts that can be initially quite confusing is the relationship between cryptocurrencies and blockchain.

Blockchain technology is the underlying force behind both Bitcoin and Ethereum, but these two projects use this technology in different ways. To understand how Ethereum implements the blockchain, however, it is helpful to have some background in Bitcoin.

Bitcoin was the first digital currency and the first application built on a blockchain platform. Today, Bitcoin is by far the most popular and well-known cryptocurrency, as well as the largest, active open blockchain in the world. As Bitcoin began to enter into the mainstream, many media outlets developed a tendency to (incorrectly) use the terms "Bitcoin" and "blockchain" almost interchangeably. Even today, many articles can be found that struggle to elucidate the relationship between Bitcoin, other cryptocurrencies, and blockchain technology.

Imagine a Google spreadsheet, one that every computer in the world shares and a spreadsheet that is connected to the internet. Each time something happens, a transaction, it will be recorded on a separate row on the spreadsheet.

Anyone who has a computer or a mobile device can log on to the internet and can see the spreadsheet. They can see every transaction that happens on the spreadsheet, and they can add another transaction if they want. The only thing they cannot do is make any changes to the transactions that are already on there.

That is, in essence, the blockchain. Nice and easy, isn't it? Where the spreadsheet has the rows, a blockchain has blocks. Each block is a collection of data, and each bit of data is added by the connection of one block to the next and so on in chronological order, pretty much the same as a spreadsheet is made up rows that follow one another. These connected blocks make a chain.

Therefore, the blockchain is a global database, online, that anyone who has an internet connection can view and use. Because this database exists on the net, it is classed as decentralized – the ledger or database is shared between every computer in the world, not just stored in one specific location with limited access.

This is what makes cryptocurrencies like Bitcoin and Ethereum so unique.

Ethereum Blockchain

Before Ethereum, blockchain based systems were mainly created to contain financial transactions. There were very few practical applications of blockchain technology outside of cryptocurrencies or finance.

While the potential of blockchain technology was starting to be realized before Ethereum, every new idea required its unique blockchain and network of computers.

To apply blockchain technology to a new idea, an entirely new blockchain would have to be created. This would require a cryptocurrency along with a network of computers contributing computing power to run the network.

The blockchain would then be specific to the purpose it was created for. A blockchain based system for financial transactions, couldn't also process transactions involving other types of data.

The Ethereum blockchain can contain contracts, computer code, and almost any type of data. Applications can be built that run on top of the Ethereum blockchain and utilize the existing computing power of the Ethereum network.

Blocks of data can't be altered or reversed, which is where the power of Ethereum can be seen across many industries. It is easy to create an application on the Ethereum blockchain, any data recorded on the blockchain will create a permanent record of that information.

Data in a block can't be altered or changed; any changes will be made in future blocks on the blockchains that are linked to the previous blocks. This creates a permanent record and an audit trail of all actions and changes that have occurred since the first entry on the blockchain.

There is no confusion as to what was originally agreed upon or the changes that have been made. Each change is timestamped and permanently recorded on the blockchain. This immutable audit trail can be applied to any application or contract.

Chapter 5: Smart Contract

The main reason for Ethereum was as a platform for smart contracts and these are run on the Ethereum Virtual Machine. This gives us a better language for scripting than Bitcoin does. Given that these contracts run in EVM, to limit the number of resources used by each contract, each operation is executed by all nodes in the network. A contract code for an Ethereum transaction triggers reads and writes of data, sends messages to other contracts, and can do some expensive computations, among other things. Each operation has a cost that is measured in gas and each of the gas units that are "eaten" by a transaction is paid for in ETH. The cost is based on a price of gas to ETH which is dynamic and constantly changing. The price is automatically deducted from the account that sends the transaction. Each transaction also has a gas limit that is bound on the amount of gas the transaction consumes. This is a safeguard against errors in programming that could deplete your account of ETH.

As Ethereum came to prominence, so did the smart contract. At its most basic level, a smart contract is nothing more than a bit of computer code that allows for contracts to be conducted by way of "self-executing" computer networks.

You can exchange just about any commodity with these hands-free contracts without having to use any intermediary. The smart contract is a true innovation and one of the primary motivators for the creation of Ethereum in the first place.

To write a smart contract, you need to know a little something about programming, but fortunately for us, we don't have to. Ethereum takes care of this for us. One neat aspect of smart contracts is their ability to signal other contracts. It works in layers. You can make one contract on the surface and then several contracts below. This just so happens to work out fabulously for the coming AI driven world of the "Internet of Things."

Ethereum uses the same blockchain infrastructure, but it opens the door for any program to be executed.

Even when we continue to think regarding financial transactions, the possibilities that Ethereum offers allow for things like conditions, creating a much more flexible environment for payment systems. For example, with Ethereum, a secure deposit could be held on the blockchain for a specified period: if a set of conditions were not met, it could be returned to the payer; if the conditions were met, the payment could be released to the payee. In Bitcoin, there is no way to hold the payment in "escrow" like this without the use of a third party. This kind of conditional transaction is a simple example of something that could be executed with a smart contract in Ethereum.

Another use case for smart contracts could include a 'multi-signature' approach to releases funds, meaning that a specified number of people must all agree to release the funds for the contract to be fulfilled. To further complicate matters, but also make them much more exciting, smart contracts are often used to trigger other smart contracts. For example, let's say you wanted to place a bet that your favorite sports team was going to win their next game: You could use one contract to place the bet, and in the background another smart contract would be used to gather data about the game and process the results, which would then send the outcome back to yet another smart contract to handle dispensing payout to the winner.

Disadvantages of smart contracts:

1. It is an untested method for creating and enforcing contracts. Legal contracts have been used for hundreds of years; they may not be perfect, but they've stood the test of time. Smart contracts are new and haven't been proven over a long period. Using smart contracts at this

early stage may expose businesses to unexpected risks associated with new technology.

2. Jurisdiction for enforcement of the smart contract can be unclear. Smart contracts are computer code that can exist without legal jurisdiction of a country or state. If there is a breach of contract or dispute about the terms of the contract, the smart contract may have no legal jurisdiction other than the blockchain. It is possible that any arbitration that may be possible would occur in a blockchain arbitration court handled by computer code, as proposed by the company CodeLegit.

3. You can't argue with a smart contract. The contract will enforce the terms based on the code. There is no judge to determine whether the terms are fair or an appeals court to challenge any decision. If a party feels the contract was unfair or was executed incorrectly due to error or a misunderstanding of the terms, there are no avenues to challenge the contract.

4. Software problems could cause errors in the smart contract. Smart contracts run on Ethereum, which relies on a network of computers and software to operate. Problems with the software or network could cause errors in smart contracts.

5. There is a limit to the types of contracts that can be created. Digital ownership of assets can be determined; however, it may be more difficult for real-world assets. It may also be difficult for smart contracts to determine whether the quality of work was up to the standard expected. Basic yes-and-no requirements could be programmed, such as, "Was one hour of work completed?" However, the quality of that work may not be able to be determined.

6. Errors in computer code could be worse than ambiguous words in a contract. If there are ambiguous words in a contract, it can be discussed, amended, debated or taken to court. If there is an error in the computer code in a contract, the contract will run the code with the error, and it can't be reversed or taken to court.

7. Lawyers are replaced with computer programmers.

Computer programmers will be required to create them instead of lawyers.

While anyone can create a smart contract, very few people will have the skills required to write one themselves.

Chapter 6: Relevant variables for smart contracts

The variables that you add to a smart contract are always going to be organized in the same fashion.

The first variable will be the address variable which refers to the location of the ether wallet that is going to be the primary account of the contract. This address is generated when the contract is created and can be found via the conference () function. The address will either be listed as the owner's or the organizer's wallet. If you use Geth, you will have the ability to generate different account addresses from a single node. If you are using this feature, then the address variable is always going to refer to the primary account that is created. Every smart contract that is created will have a pair of addresses, the first being the wallet address and the second is the address of the contract after it is deployed. You can gain access to the contract address directly via the primary Solidity interface through the command contract: address myaddress=this.

The second variable in the UINIT variable which is an abbreviation for an unsigned integer. This variable is listed as 256.

The third variable is going to be either PRIVATE OR PUBLIC which will determine if the smart contract you have created is going to be able to access information outside the blockchain directly through the use of what is known as an oracle. If outside information is required then this will be set to public, otherwise private will suffice.

The next two variables are ARRAYS and MAPPING which Solidity will automatically generate details for. To change these presets, you will need to use the command address=>unit. You will need to make sure that your overall contract footprint and any related information is as small as possible. These variables are ultimately used to determine who has to pay for what after specific variables are achieved.

Calls

A call function is a call that changes the way the current contract operates through modifying existing records or adding new records to an exciting set. This can also be done through the Web3.js function as it can be used to move variables around in a specific smart contract.

These variables can be determined beforehand through the use of Solidty, more specifically the msg.sender and msg.value commands. Altering either of the resulting variables will alter where the funds are coming from and how much will reach the account designated to receive them.

Suicide button

It is important to always include a suicide option in your smart contracts that will allow them to self-destruct when needed. This is important if you accidentally make a mistake and a transfer doesn't go through properly then the only way to get the transaction out of limbo is to destroy the contract and start again. Once destroyed, the funds will return to their primary wallet.

Chapter 7: Ethereum wallet

Creating an Ethereum wallet

There are a ton of Ethereum wallets. Google Chrome plugin and Firefox Add-on Metamask are   recommended. Https://github.com/MetaMask/metamask-plugin can make you see the code since the software is open source. A secure wallet will be present in your browser where you can send and receive Ethereum very quickly. This wallet can be used in the acceptance of Ethereum.

1. Get the add-on. If you are on Firefox, go to https://addons.mozilla.org/en-US/firefox/addon/ether-metamask/. If you are in Chrome, go to https://metamask.io/ then click on "Get Chrome Extension."

2. When installing MetaMask, "Add to Chrome" should be clicked as an extension of Google Chrome (left image below) or click "Add to Firefox" for Firefox users (right image below).

3. Once installed, you will see a fox icon in your browser bar up top. Click on it and accept terms of use.

4. Create a new vault. This typically will be your wallet. You will need to enter and store a strong password. Like our wallet advice above, make sure you can safely store this password. Anyone with this password will be able to drain your wallet of any coins! You will need to rely on the 12-word seed phrase you set up next.

5. Archive your backup 12-word seed phrase. You will be shown your 12-word seed phrase in the app. This is the most important bit of information for you to record and keep safe when managing your MetaMask account.

If you need to install MetaMask onto another computer or have to restore a crashed computer, you will need these 12 words! As we noted above, before you put money into MetaMask, you could try and delete the plugin and then try to restore it with your seed phrase.

You can write your seed phrase down on a piece of paper, store it on a flash drive or we also make it optional to download a file containing this information.

6. Wallet ready for transactions! Here is a wallet I created. Make sure you have selected the Main Network in the upper right hand. See arrow below.

There are test networks we want to avoid. You can click on the three dots to get your Wallet address by selecting "Copy Address to Clipboard." You will see your balance where I have blocked off below in black.

This means you are on the live Ripple network and all transactions will be recorded.

An Ethereum wallet consists of a few main components:

•   Ethereum address: This is similar to an email address. You provide your Ethereum address to other people, so they can send you Ether, just like you would provide your email address to other people so that they can email you.

Your Ethereum address is public. Everyone on the Ethereum network can view your balance and all transactions that have occurred on your address.

An Ethereum wallet can hold multiple addresses.

•   Client / Software: To access your wallet and make transactions, you will need software or a way to access your wallet and communicate with the Ethereum network. This is known as the client, which may be a mobile app, website, or computer software that connects to the network.

This is similar to how you would access your bank account and make transactions using the mobile app or website for your bank.

•   Private Key: A private key is a password used to prove ownership of your Ethereum address to access it and transfer Ether from the address.

Chapter 8: Wallet Types

Storing Ether in Wallets

The best place to store all those hard-won units of Ethereum is in a wallet. Not the physical kind mind you, we are talking about a wallet that solely resides in cyberspace. The wallet is the online repository of your addresses, or as they are referred to, "private keys." These keys consist of a long string of numbers and letters chosen at random and serve as the password to unlock your stash in Ethereum.

Putting Your Wallet into Various forms of Cold Storage

It's because of this risk that some prefer to store their wallets completely in cold storage. What's cold storage? Cold storage simply refers to any information stored offline. If you have files and keys for your wallet stored on a thumb drive that has never been exposed to the internet, it is in cold storage.

One means of keeping a wallet safe from the ravages of the internet is through the use of the "paper wallet." Paper wallets are—just as you might imagine—simply pieces of paper that you scrawled your Ethereum addresses onto. Since these addresses are kept away from the internet, they are not at risk of being compromised. These private keys are safely removed from the dangers of cyberspace.

Another no-brainer in the quest for offline storage is the "brain wallet" this method entails simply memorizing your wallet info in your brain! Yes, for the more memory gifted among us, if you can simply memorize the keys to your Ethereum wallet you would be all the better for it!

Hardware Wallet

Hardware wallets are stand-alone units that you can plug into your device to store private keys for your Ethereum. As long as the device is offline, there is no threat of any of your keys becoming compromised. Transactional signatures can be placed on the device while it is offline before you plug the hardware wallet in again. This way the only time you are open to any risk is when the device is plugged in. And if you have a good antivirus program even this risk can be mitigated.

Hardware wallets must be connected to a computer to send transactions, which may expose them to some security risks. Hardware wallets are designed, so the private key is not exposed when sending transactions. Some hardware wallets may allow you to hide wallets with large balances, in case of theft or a situation where you are forced to expose the balance of your hardware wallet.

Paper Wallet

A paper wallet is a wallet printed on a piece of paper. The piece of paper will contain the public address and QR code for the wallet, which can be provided to other people to send money to that wallet. When a paper wallet is printed, it may also have the private key on it. Make sure you remove the private key and keep the private key separate.

Paper wallets are not connected to a computer, website, or electronic network, so they are not vulnerable to many risks of software or web-based wallets. Paper wallets can't be hacked and provide a cold storage option for securely storing Ether.

Chrome Extensions

Chrome extensions are applications that run on the Google Chrome web browser. They can do almost anything a website or software can do and are accessible from the menu bar of a web browser.

There are Ethereum wallet chrome extensions that allow you to send and receive Ether from within your web browser. An advantage of chrome extensions is they can provide enhanced functionality to websites you visit by detecting Ether addresses on pages or connecting to web apps.

Software wallet

Software installed from the internet may pose higher security risks than a mobile app, so be careful to check where you are downloading the software from.

Software wallets can run on computer and laptop monitors, so they have a larger, easier to use design compared to mobile. They may also allow you to hold multiple cryptocurrencies and tokens within your wallet.

Software wallet allows you to install and manage an Ethereum wallet from your computer or laptop. They are a little more difficult to install and set up; however, if you've ever installed computer software, you should have no problem installing them.

Mobile Apps

Mobile apps are easy to install and use, like any other mobile app. They provide the convenience of having access to your cryptocurrency wallet in your smartphone and are more secure than other options, as they must pass security requirements set by the app stores.

Hybrid Web Wallet / Exchange

A hybrid web wallet/exchange combines the features of an Ethereum web wallet with an exchange. It provides the ability to send and receive Ether like a web wallet, along with buying or selling Ether at exchange market prices.

Hybrid web wallets/exchanges allow you to purchase Ether using traditional payment methods, such as bank accounts and credit cards. They are regulated similar to other financial institutions and require verification of identity before you can make purchases.

Exchange

With an exchange, you can hold many cryptocurrencies in the same account and trade between them easily. They are regulated, like financial institutions. They may also have features, such as customer support and security methods, similar to traditional online banking websites.

You don't control your private keys with an exchange. While this reduces the chance of you losing your private keys, it opens you up to other risks, such as the exchange being hacked or going bankrupt. This occurred with the largest Bitcoin exchange Mt.Gox. While it is less of a risk now, as exchanges are more regulated, the risk still exists.

Web Wallet

A web wallet is a wallet that can be accessed from a web browser on a computer or mobile. It is similar to logging into internet banking in a web browser on your computer.

Beginners can use web wallets or experienced cryptocurrency users. They can be set up in minutes from a web browser with no ID verification required.

Web wallets require no applications or software to be installed. The website does any updates to the web wallet on their servers, so you need not update or download new versions of the web wallet.

Web wallets provide you access to your private keys. There is no customer service or company to contact if you lose your private keys. Make sure you backup your private keys and take care of them; otherwise, you will lose access to your web wallet.

Get Your Ethereum Client

Working in tandem with your Ethereum wallet is your Ethereum client program. You will find quite a plethora of clients, each written in their unique scripting language. Several evaluators are then used to determine their veracity. It may take a bit of experimentation to figure out what might work best for you, but there should be a client out there that fits your needs. An Ethereum client can help make your whole experience with Ethereum complete.

Using a Hybrid Wallet

The wallet that truly seems to have the best of both worlds when it comes to convenience and security is the "Hybrid Wallet." This wallet makes use of both hot and cold storage by having a device that goes online and conducts transactions, along with a separate device that stays offline and is simply used to store private keys. The keys are made offline, so they don't come into contact with the internet until you decide to use them The Hybrid Wallet is a great option to keep your Ethereum secure. If you need a good mix of structure and facilitation, the hybrid wallet is the way to go.

Chapter 9: Ethereum Mining

While the mining of bitcoin is all the rage in certain sectors these days, the cryptocurrency king isn't the only one of its kind to utilize the help of the masses when it comes to verifying transactions. Rather, every cryptocurrency that uses a proof-of-work model uses more or less the same process. Mining is accomplished via the use of high powered computers, or mining machines, that use a version of the SHA-256 mining process to uphold the sanctity and security of the blockchain. The speed with which a given machine can validate transactions is determined in hashes per second.

Ethereum mining is the act of accruing ETH tokens by validating transactions on the network. Specifically, it is the participation in validating all transactions that happen to ensure all Ethereum blockchain activity is confirmed. Ethereum mining can be done on pretty much any platform, making it available to the home computer user, not just those with expensive tailored mining rigs. It does tend to be easier if you have a UNIX computer, rather than Windows though, where Ethereum is concerned.

The biggest challenge with mining Ethereum is to generate more value in ETH token than the mining costs regarding electricity. As a newbie, your very best chance of generating ETH through mining is to get involved in a mining pool, and I will talk a little more about those later.

Mining ether is one way to make money on the Ethereum network. If you want to get started as a miner, the first thing that you will need is a powerful enough computer and a GPU card. You will need to download the Ethereum mining software, which is free, and connect it to a wallet. You will also want to make sure that you have a source of cheap energy so that the mining is profitable, as it does use a lot of energy. The best form of energy for mining is solar or wind, as this is not only significantly cheaper than traditional fossil fuels but also promotes sustainability of the network. You will probably want to join a mining pool, which will increase your probability of solving the algorithms and getting paid in the ether.

The Ethereum Mining Algorithm

Before 2016, Proof-of-work was the mining algorithm used on Ethereum and the process mirrored that of Bitcoin quite closely. After 2016, when the switch was made to the Casper Proof of Stake algorithm, a lot of things changed in Ethereum mining. It became a lot easier to validate transactions and the time lag reduced tremendously. It has always been clear to many Cryptocurrency and Blockchain experts that Proof-of-Work was fundamentally flawed in some ways and a better transaction verification system was needed, one that vastly improved speed and reduced energy consumption in the process. Casper is just one of the successful implementations of this paradigm shift in the Blockchain sphere.

How to Get Involved Ethereum Mining

In Ethereum Mining Pools, miners join with a network of other miners thus increasing their probability of being able to acquire Ether by successfully validating transaction blocks. There are many Ethereum Mining Pool configurations adopted by several Ethereum Mining Pools.

Even though there have been concerted efforts to ensure that entry cost into Ethereum mining is kept at a minimum, it would not necessarily be a wise idea to try and start mining Ether on your own. Just like in the Bitcoin Network, joining a pool of miners is still the better option. There are two main options for anyone wishing to explore this option, and these options are Ethereum Mining Pools and Ethereum Cloud Mining. Most of these configurations are based on the method used to distribute revenue within the network. The most popular configurations are Proportional Payouts (PROP) and Pay per Share (PPS). In recent times, there has also been a new configuration that is becoming increasingly popular, and it called the Double Geometric Method (DGM).

Ethereum Cloud Mining is a lot like Bitcoin Cloud Mining in the sense that it involves entering into a mining contract with a Cloud Mining service provider. There are various forms of Ethereum Cloud Mining, and they include Virtual Hosted Mining, Leased Hashing Power and Hosted Mining Services. As is the case with Bitcoin, some Ethereum Cloud Mining service providers are internet scams.

Hardware

If you have ever had a slow PC, you have probably executed this command to see why your computer's processing speed is running so slow. With the task manager pulled up you can browse through all the commands and processes being carried out by your system's CPU. For a PC that has become overwhelmed with too many tasks to process, the overall runtime of the system will slow down. It is for this reason that you might find yourself closing out programs in your task manager. It's so you can give your overloaded CPU some much-needed breathing space.

With all of the items on the plate for a CPU today, most are just not capable of handling the extra burden of mining for Ethereum, and even if they are, the tortoise-like speed with which they do it would not be worth the effort. It is for this reason that better, faster hardware is required. It was for this purpose that the utilization of the graphic processing unit or "GPU" hardware mining computers first came in vogue. Since a GPU's bread and butter is to process graphics, utilizing GPU's for mining at first presented a significant improvement.

Cloud-Based Mining for Ether

The utilization of powerful cloud-based processors can greatly increase the speed with which ether is mind. It will also alleviate the strain on our hardware and lower your utility bills in the process. By using a cloud-based mining rig, you can also free yourself from having to do any maintenance on your operation since it is all handled in the cloud. Amazon EC2 is currently the most popular cloud-based mining group being used to mine for Ether, as well as Bitcoin.

Join an Ethereum Mining Pool

With such a massive interest in mining for Ethereum, going it alone in the world of mining could render you some rather slim pickings. It is for this reason that Ethereum enthusiasts have decided to band together and join forces in what is known as "mining pools." Joining such a pool in your quest for Ethereum will allow you to not only increase the speed with which your ether is mined, but it will also save you on precious resources such as electricity!

By joining an Ethereum mining pool, you can save yourself much of the burden and expense that you would otherwise engender.

Chapter 10: Ethereum Programming

To create your app on the Ethereum platform, you are going to want to use the Solidity programing language which is similar to JavaScript. It uses both the .sol and the .se extension in addition to LLL, the byproduct of Lisp. If you have even used Python or Serpent, then Solidity is sure to feel familiar, and users from both are switching to Solidity on a regular basis.

To easily compile the apps and smart contracts that you create, you will need to use a variation of the solc compiler that uses C++. If you prefer not to go the solc route, you can instead use a browser-based alternative such as Cosmo, though this chapter will assume you went with the solc complier. Furthermore, once you have compiled your work you are going to need to use the Ethereum Web3.ja API to utilize the JavaScript that will connect the smart contract to the app. This will ultimately allow you to interact with your smart contracts directly without forcing you to log into an Ethereum node to do so.

Distributed application framework

Numerous complex frameworks have already been created by like-minded developers that have been released to the Ethereum community for free with the goal of developing community output as a whole. One of these is a great place to start without having to worry about building your framework from the ground up.

Embark/Truffle

Truffle is a great framework to start with as it automates several of the more generic steps in the programming process as a means of developing distributed applications more readily by providing developers more free time to work on deploying, compiling and testing the best code they can manage. Embark typically comes in handy when building and streamlining apps by automating much of the testing process.

Events

Depending on the ultimate use of the smart contract in question, it will need to include various events including receiving or sending funds that will be listed in the events log section of the smart contract that can be found connected to the block that the transaction ends up being attached to. This variable won't change what the smart contract is up to; it just makes all the details easier to reference.

APIs

The most common decentralized API is that which was created by BlockApps.net. It mimics a normal Ethereum node if you are not in a position to run a real one at the moment. A common alternative is called MetaMask which makes it easy to run the standard array of Ethereum platform tools on any web browser. Another option is LightWallet which is an easy way for users and developers to interact with decentralized apps with different interfaces for each group of users.

Meteor

When it comes to improving the stack, Meteor, which naturally works with the Web3.js API, is the choice of many Ethereum developers. It also works like a standard web application framework as well. Meteor is one of the leading supporters of the Ethereum platform as was discussed heavily at the November 2016 Ethereum Development Conference.

Chapter 11: Build your app

1.   The initial thing you will be required to do to build an app successfully is to formulate an Ethereum node to work from. The certified way to go about doing so is through Geth, the Ethereum node interface.

a.   From the command line, enter bash<(curlhttps://install-geth.ethereum.org)

b. Next, you will be advised to start the Geth installation; you will require to select the suitable operating system along with the latest version of the Ethereum CLL.

c. After the installation has finished favorably, you will then be free to interact with Geth through an environment based on JavaScript along with standard console commands. Specialized console commands will be saved between situations to allow you to track your progress more easily.

d. All that is left at this point is to get to work. Open a terminal tool as a means of opening the Geth console. After the program launches you should see a less than sign as an indication that things are working properly. To quit, you simply type exit at that point and press the ENTER key.

e. The Geth console will automatically redirect or log output to the console if you use the command gethconsole2>>geth.log. You will also be able to access this log via the command tail-fgeth.log.

2.   The next thing you are going to do, after creating the smart contract or decentralized application in question, is to compile it using the solc C++ compiler.

3.   Once everything has been compiled, you will now be ready to deploy your results. To do so, you are going to need to pay a gas fee and also digitally sign a contract. After this is done, you will then receive access to a specific address that houses the contract in the blockchain as well as the ABI for your new product.

4.   Once you have the ABI, you will then be able to check on the application or contract from any device that is connected to the internet. Depending on what your creation does exactly, each time you interact with it you may need to pay a gas fee.

Testing

If you are creating a smart contract, then it is important that your if/then statements are constructed in such a way that there is no room for questioning whether or not specific qualifications are met. This is where Truffle comes into play as it will automatically generate the type of framework that JavaScript and Web3.js need to make this type of code work correctly.

Test the transaction time

The promises that you decide to utilize are going to be a crucial part of whether your smart contract or app sees use as it is going to take at least 10 seconds for your contract to be verified, and that is just the speed that is attainable under perfect testing conditions. When you are ready to begin testing your contract, you are going to need to head to the test directory and change the extension on the .js file to conference.js and also change any other references as well. After this, all you are going to need to do is run Truffle in the root directory that holds your test file. With this done you will then:

1.   Begin by opening Pip, Solidity and solc. You will want to ensure your main library is separated from your test library by using a virtual environment.

2.   Once this is done, you are going to need to open the console window and start a new node

client. You will need to start Truffle and then use the deploy command to activate the standard init that can be used with smart contracts. Doing so will also allow the program to point out any errors that the code may contain at this point.

3.   As you develop your code, it is always a good idea to test the compilation in Truffle to ensure that you aren't taken by surprise when you go to compile the final version. Truffle will also allow you to test the deployment of contracts in a test space as well.

Deployment

Once you have successfully tested your contract, you can then deploy it from Truffle directly. To go about doing so:

1.   Start by opening the console and using the code truffle init (new directory) to generate a new directory.

2.   Locate the contract you have created; it will be listed as name.solc.

3.   Open the app.json/config file and type in the name of your new contract under the space for Contracts.

4.   Start up your Ethereum node, open another window in the console before using the tesrpc command.

5.   With that done you will then need to rerun Truffle and choose the option to deploy from the root directory.

Chapter 12: Dealing with DApps

Ethereum makes use of several decentralized apps—better known as DApps which help facilitate activity on the network. DApps are relatively new on the scene, but they nevertheless have been a game changer, creating several fascinating innovations within the overall framework of Ethereum. The integral traits of a good DApp are that they are; open source, decentralized, incentivized, and they should meet some protocol. That they should be decentralized is rather obvious.

But what surprises some is that DApps are open source, meaning that anyone can change them at will. But the thing is—these changes will not go into effect unless a consensus among users has been reached that recognizes the value and need to enact that change.

Augur

Augur is a mightily powerful DApp because it seeks t bring together the ideas in the more speculative marketplace with the tremendous reach presented by a blockchain which stretches across the breadth of an entirely decentralized Ethereum-based ecosystem. This is creating the perfect storm for the advent of what investors refer to as a "super-forecaster" that is capable of navigating through the more turbulent waters for tremendous profit and reward.

The Golem Project

The long-term aim and stated goal of its creators are to connect all the devices on the planet to create a truly decentralized internet. This may not occur for a while yet, but in the meantime, this DApp is wildly popular for Ethereum enthusiasts.

This DApp first came into being a couple of years ago and has in the meantime Ethereum enthusiasts have been chomping at the bit to get investors to devote some of their PC's processing power to this DApp. This is to create a network of decentralized computers to makeup one giant virtual machine.

BAT DAap

These DAap's are designed to make your life easier, not harder, so don't make things harder than it is. It is up to Ethereum user whether they choose to allow this personal data mining on their behalf, and if they choose to do so, they will be compensated with more opportunity to shine on the blockchain. Use BAT DAap to streamline your whole experience with Ethereum.

It sounds almost like some dipping sauce made up of ground bat meat, but I can assure you, a BAT DAap is nothing of the sort. Standing for "Basic Attention Token," a BAT is used to quite literally get the word out. BAT utilizes a special private internet browser to follower all transactions. This is done with complete anonymity, making sure that no personally identifying information is ever leaked out, even while specific user data is sent through a secure channel back to potential marketers.

Status

For those of you who enjoy keeping up with your Ethereum investments by way of your mobile phone, the Status DAap should be of particular interest to you. With this DAap you can transform your entire phone into one standalone node of the Ethereum ecosystem. This is beneficial to you because as long as you have your mobile converted node, you will have instant access to Ethereum network in its entirety. This DAap also serves to streamline all smart contracts and all other transactions that are carried out among users.

Melonport

This helpful little DApp helps to facilitate digital asset management. Those who use it can create their strategic managerial methods. The Melonport DAap makes the most of the technological advancement of blockchain and uses it to foster healthy competition and dialogue between users. And in a very realistic business sense, it helps to lower cost and removes barriers that could limit your investing options. But even better than all this, Melonport takes full advantage of the open source nature of Ethereum, allowing users to participate in real-world feedback.

Chapter 13: Investing in Cryptocurrencies

2016 was the year the cryptocurrency market really exploded and now there are various types of all shapes and sizes floating around in the investment markets. While bitcoin still has the greatest price and the largest trading volume, Ethereum still saw a respective 300 percent growth last year. This doesn't mean that investing in ether is without risk, however, which is why it is important to keep in mind the pros and cons outlined here prior to making any investment decisions.

When someone bought their first Ether on January 26th, 2016, they had to pay a just a little over 0.006 BTC for one Ethereum. After just two weeks, this price appreciated in value to the tune of 0.017 BTC as of the second week in February. That's a 300% return in just two a few weeks' time making this Ethereum currency look like a very lucrative part of any portfolio.

That initial Ether bubble burst shortly afterward but has continued to grow, as of September 17th, 2016 the price for one Ethereum is 0.0208 BTC, and it remains the second largest CC as far as market capitalization, with Bitcoin in a strong lead. This is an impressive result for an 8-month old CC and with the benefits outlined above; there is clearly a larger market to be captured, and a larger growth to be had in the future.

The following are some top tips for those new to investing in cryptocurrencies.

• Altcoin Trading

Never forget about the power of the altcoin. Bitcoin is not the only cryptocurrency in the world and the altcoins are not quite so prone to the public speculation. They have much smaller market caps which are more prone to bigger pricing swings but each one has its own purpose, and it has intent. The risks of investing with altcoins are bigger, but the rewards can also be much bigger too. Some, like Ethereum, are more stable while some are at a higher risk of fluctuation so allocate your percentages per your risk tolerance. For example, you could put say 50% into Bitcoin, 30% into Ethereum, 15% into DASH and 5% in ZCash

There are plenty of rules and tips for investing but, on the whole, where cryptocurrency is concerned, you can get away with following the same guidelines as for other investments.

- Understand Just How Powerful Cryptocurrency Is

We tend to look at this the same way as we do when we invest in stocks, but cryptocurrencies are commodities, not stocks. Yes, both have a price, but they are very different with the only real similarity being the exchange. We already know that the blockchain technology that backs Bitcoin is being studied for the potential to change retail and institutional capital and the decentralized nature of cryptocurrency means that there is no way to shut it down and no way to manipulate it easily. When people ask why you want to invest in cryptocurrencies like Bitcoin, you can tell them that it is the safest investment anyone can make and that you believe in the future – for as long as Bitcoin capital continues to flow, its potential will continue to be realized.

- Start Small

One of the ways to cut risk in sudden changes with Bitcoin and other cryptocurrencies is to average the dollar cost of your purchase. This takes the sting out of sudden changes in pricing and cuts your reliance on a single entry point. Increasing your investment over time you cut out the need to buy and sell too often. Cryptocurrencies are here to stay, so there is no need to go all out and fill the coffers straight away – unless of course, the prices drop to all-time lows!

- Always Have a Strategy

How often are you going to buy and sell? There are those that just want to be day traders, but it has already been shown that your best bet could be to hold. The rule of thumb is that the longer you hold, the less risk there is, and this rule works for cryptocurrency investments as well. However, sometimes it will be better to cut loose and get out, and one of the indicators for that is when unforeseen structural issues cause declines in price. Always make sure you have a strategy in place that covers all eventualities.

- Hedging Your Bets

Some exchanges are happy to allow short orders – this lets you place a bet on either side of the price movements. For example, you could go 10% short and 90% long which would assume you have far more confidence in the long run. This kind of strategy can cater to all risk levels.

Chapter 14: Investing In Ethereum

Should you invest in Ethereum?

Investors all over the world are getting into Ethereum. China, in particular, has been very committed. What's their motivation? There are quite a few reasons why Ethereum is such a good choice, and you need to understand them before investing yourself:

1. Ethereum is used in the real world

Investors care about if the thing they're interested in is being used in the real world. Real-world usage proves that people want and need it, so there's a good chance the investment is going to stay stable, and demand will increase. Based on supply and demand data, investors have found that Ethereum is indeed actually being used. This is in large part because Ethereum is so popular with dapp creators, who use ether as their fuel.

2. The price of ether is going to keep going up

This is a matter of opinion, and many investors say that ether is in a bubble and headed for a crash. If you don't already know, a "bubble" is the term used for when the price of something goes up dramatically and steadily, so it starts to cost more than it's worth. This foreshadows a sudden crash and the bubble bursts.

However, there are others who say that because of the nature of Ethereum, a bubble and subsequent crash isn't even really a possibility. This is because as more dapps are created using Ethereum, the price of ether will go up. Because there is no limit to the number and scope of dapps, that could mean there isn't a limit to ether's growth either!

3. Security is built in

Security is king these days, with so many hacks and leaks, and Ethereum has a system that encourages security. All the code that approves transactions is kept on all the nodes in the Ethereum system, not a single authority, so hacking is very difficult. All the nodes act as checks on each other. While it is true that Ethereum had that huge DAO hack, the fact that it recovered so quickly and is still so successful is very important. It shows that when something goes wrong in the system, it is possible to correct it.

4.   It's pretty stable

Even though Ethereum has been very volatile, experts say this is perfectly normal and healthy, and compared to over crypto coins, ether has not seen spikes extreme enough to cause concern. This makes Ethereum a relatively stable investment. Despite the DAO hack, demand is still high and shows people have faith in Ethereum as a platform.

5. It has long-term potential

Ethereum has much potential in so many areas, like healthcare and identity management. Even as the price of ether rises and falls, the future is going to be using blockchain and Ethereum-based smart contracts, so it only makes sense to put one's money into it now, even if it goes through ups and downs.

Chapter 15: Popular Ethereum exchanges

Bitfinex

With more than 200,000 trades a week, Bitfinex is the most popular cryptocurrency exchange on the market today. This is an exchange that lets you trade without verification if you already have cryptocurrency in hand.

Coinbase

This the longest lasting cryptocurrency exchange that has been in continuous operation on the market today. It is extremely well regulated and is one of the top five exchanges with the highest daily volume.

Bitstamp

This is another elder statesman of the cryptocurrency exchanges, having first opened in 2011. It is the second most popular exchange and sees more than 10,000 trades every day.

OKCoin

This exchange is great for those who are looking for fewer regulations but still want to trade

USD. This exchange is based in China so most of the rules that traditionally govern exchanges do not apply.

Kraken

This is one of the top 15 most popular exchanges that trades in USD and is also the most popular exchange that deals in euros. It also offers a number of smaller cryptocurrencies for trading, though only in limited trading pairs.

Chapter 16: ICOs and Ethereum Tokens

ICOs have become a popular way for companies and developers to raise money to fund development of applications or businesses. In this chapter, we'll cover what ICOs are, how they work, and their dangers.

What is an ICO?

ICO is an acronym for "Initial Coin Offering." It is when developers or a company raise money by offering a new coin or token for purchase. This may be a new cryptocurrency or a token on the Ethereum platform that can be used in an application.

We'll cover how ICOs work later in this chapter, but first, we'll cover Ethereum tokens to understand what is being offered in an ICO.

A majority of ICO funding seems to be coming from China these days, though investors from across the globe have been known to jump in on the ground floor if the price is right. Besides the conventional wisdom that goes along with investing in an untested commodity, ICOs have their issues which make them extra risky. The biggest of these is the fact that the Securities and Exchange Commission is currently looking into whether ICOs are avoiding regulations that would require them to have to meet the same standards as IPOs. There is also a fear that the current round of ICO success has created a bubble around the market that can only be sustained for so long.

How ICOs work

The developers can raise money for the app to pay wages, without selling shares in a company or borrowing money.

Gas Price and Gas Limit

Applications to an ICO are treated like transactions to a smart contract. They are processed by miners that receive a fee for processing the transaction.

Gas Price and Gas Limit determine the fee the miner receives. The higher the gas price and gas limit you set on a transaction, the faster the transaction will be processed.

During an ICO, the transaction fees paid are much higher, as people want to ensure their transactions are processed faster so they don't miss out if the ICO sells out quickly. The ICO website will usually have a recommended Gas Limit and Gas Price to send. They may also set a maximum limit to create a fairer offer, ensuring people aren't forced to pay high transaction fees to participate.

If an application is rejected, the transaction fees are still paid, so be careful sending too many transactions or setting the fees above the recommended ICO limit.

Dangers / Risks of ICOs

There are significant risks of participating in an ICO, which we'll cover in this section.

Loss of initial investment

Perhaps the biggest risk is the loss of the money you invest in the ICO. This could be due to several reasons. While you may be aware losing your investment is a risk, it is the reasons you may lose your money you may be unaware of.

The tokens don't go up in value

If the developers create an app and people use it, there is still the risk the tokens don't go up in value.

There may have been a lot of tokens sold in the ICO, which creates an excessive supply of tokens. While people may use the app, the demand for tokens may not be enough to increase the price of the tokens.

The app is not popular

Even if the developers can create an app, there is no guarantee the app will be popular or that anyone will want to use the app.

If very few people are using the app, then the tokens won't go up in value and may even fall in value. Over time, the tokens may become worthless, as nobody wants to use the app; therefore, nobody needs to buy the tokens.

Developers never create an app

Many ICOs raise money to fund the development of an application. There is no guarantee they will build an app. Creating software is time-consuming and costly, and the developers may run out of money before they can create anything.

Legal and regulatory risks

China has recently banned ICOs and moved to close cryptocurrency exchanges. Part of the ban on ICOs that China implemented was for any companies that raised funds via an ICO to return funds to the people that purchased tokens.

There are guidelines and rules in most countries about creating companies and offering shares to investors, and ICOs attempt to get around these regulations.

While ICOs have been allowed so far, this is mainly due to the fact they are a new technology where regulation doesn't yet exist. The Securities and Exchange Commission (SEC) in the U.S with financial regulatory institutions in other countries are examining ICOs with companies that raise funds via ICOs and will likely implement the regulation.

While companies may raise funds now in an ICO, they may face legal and regulatory issues in the future. These regulations may be applied retrospectively, as in China, which may affect any companies that raised funds through an ICO in the past. This could cause companies to lose money and tokens for their apps to become worthless.

Incorrect address or wallet

Another risk of applying for ICOs is sending and receiving funds. If you send funds to or from the wrong address, you may lose your funds.

If the wallet or address you put to receive the tokens isn't the correct type, you may also lose your funds.

Most ICOs require a special type of Ethereum wallet that allows you to hold tokens within the wallet. Often, the address you send funds from is the address tokens will be sent to. If this is an address that can't hold tokens, when the tokens are sent, they will be lost.

No secondary market

It is easy for a company to create a token and offer it to the public. Once you buy those tokens in an ICO, there is no guarantee you can sell them again to get your money back.

If you can't sell your tokens, then you can't get your money back or profit from them. You may only use them in an app, which is only possible if the developers create an app in the first place.

Sending Ether to an ICO

If you hold Ether in MyEtherWallet or MetaMask wallets mentioned earlier, you may receive the tokens onto the same address.

Generally, the process is that, once the ICO opens, they will provide an address, and you can send Ether to that address.

Tokens in an ICO are usually limited, and when all the tokens are sold, the ICO is complete. This often results in many transactions at the start of ICO, causing delays in the transaction times.

Scams

While there are many legitimate companies raising money in ICOs, there are also a large number of outright scams.

There are no regulations for companies raising funds using ICOs. This has allowed scammers to create websites and steal money from people unaware of the difference between a legitimate ICO and a scam.

Scammers have created websites and social media accounts that copy legitimate ICOs. This has created confusion on which is the real company, leading many people to send money to the wrong company.

Even ICOs that seem unique and legitimate may be set up by people with no intention of using money raised to build applications. They may just raise the money for themselves and claim the project or company failed. As there is no regulation, there is nothing stopping people from doing this and no legal ramifications.

Participating in an ICO

If after reading all those risks, you still want to participate in an ICO, you must be careful to do it correctly. In this section, we'll cover the wallet required and understand the basics of applying for an ICO.

Wallet required to apply for an ICO

You need a special wallet that allows you to hold tokens when applying for an ICO.

Exchanges, such as Poloniex and kraken, with hybrid web wallets, such as Coinbase, don't allow you to receive tokens from an ICO. Do not send Bitcoin or Ethereum from these platforms, as you will lose your funds and not receive your tokens.

To apply for an ICO, you will need a wallet from a site or software such as:

My Ether Wallet - myetherwallet.com

Meta Mask - metamask.io

These wallets allow you to send Ether and receive and hold tokens. Other wallets allow you to send Ether and receive tokens; however, the above are the most common wallets recommended on ICO websites.

Don't send funds before the ICO opens

ICOs will have a countdown time before the ICO starts. They will usually not release the address to send funds to before the ICO opens.

Sometimes, the address will be released a few hours before to give people time to prepare; however, any applications sent before the official opening time will not be accepted, and funds may be lost.

Chapter 17: The Future uses of Ethereum

The value of Ether reached record highs in 2017, and many speculate that the value will continue to trend upwards over time. Many major companies have adopted the Ethereum vision of a flexible blockchain platform with the ability to utilize smart contracts. As the promise of blockchain technology becomes clearer on a global scale, a surge of entrepreneurs has emerged seeking to integrate this technology into every field from energy to healthcare to politics.

Given the number of governments and companies interested in Ethereum, it is a reasonable prediction that major governments and companies will use Ethereum. Even if the companies in this alliance decide they won't be using Ethereum, there are thousands of other companies not involved in this alliance looking to utilize Ethereum in their businesses.

Although no one ever said it was a competition, many people want to know if the resurgent Ethereum will indeed someday overtake Bitcoin. And if you wanted make a wager, many experts are betting that Ethereum will indeed surpass Bitcoin by late 2018. As of this writing (late 2017) Bitcoin is still worth substantially more than Ethereum, but Ethereum's worth is accelerating at such a rapid pace, it is quite possible that it could catch up if not overtake Bitcoin before the end of 2018.

Decentralized Internet

Of all the potential that Ethereum may offer, the most revolutionary may be the ability to replace the structure of the internet with a decentralized internet.

The benefits of decentralized apps and servers were covered earlier in the book. To quickly recap this information, when you access a website, you are accessing it from a central server. All the files, photos, and data you upload are stored on that central server. If that central server is hacked, all data on that central server is vulnerable. If the server goes offline, then the website and all data are also offline.

Ethereum allows websites, applications, and almost anything you can access online today to become decentralized. These websites, apps, and data are stored and accessed from a network of decentralized computers across the world.

This has the potential to replace web hosting companies, file storage companies, and the very structure of the internet. This would create a decentralized internet controlled by individuals, not by large corporations or governments.

Financial services

The financial service industry is already taking direct steps to make Ethereum a part of all infrastructure moving forward. The Enterprise Ethereum Alliance is racing towards a scenario where the Ethereum platform houses a secondary blockchain that is specifically tailored to the needs of the financial and other industrial sectors. Additionally, smart contracts are going to continue to see an increase in use when it comes to managing workflow and a variety of approval processes that are inherent in processes such as trade clearing and the generation of settlements. Smart contracts will also be used when it comes to determining coupon payments amounts and in the generation of bonds at the point of expiration.

Smart contracts are also starting to see use in the payment of insurance claims after a specific set of binary factors have been met or avoided. With additional refinement, this type of smart contract would essentially be able to take insurance adjusters out of the system completely. The need for personal assessment would be minimized as smart cars would be able to relay all possible data directly to the insurance blockchain to ensure that facts would always hold sway. Insurance companies would also be able to increase or decrease rates automatically based on predetermined driver statistics.

Increase the adoption of electric cars

Tesla is allegedly working with the Ethereum platform to develop a means of utilizing the blockchain to allow those with electric vehicles to pull up to charging stations and plugin without having to enter any payment or identification information whatsoever manually. Each car will be linked to a specific smart contract that will be linked to a bank account and monitor the consumption of energy of the vehicle and charge the account accordingly.

Healthcare

In the field of healthcare, smart contracts are already making headway when it comes to increasing how patients and their data stay connected. Preliminary usage results from hospital testing indicate that linking patients and their charts together via a blockchain would decrease the likelihood of clerical errors by as much as 40 percent, with that number increasing even more if a serious emergency is thrown into the mix.   .

The Ethereum platform is also being put to use for potentially tracking medical studies with those in the study having their data transferred automatically for collection and then automatically paying them for their time when the study comes to an end. Perhaps unsurprisingly, a version of this same technology is also on its way to a wide variety of personal internet devices such as those that track fitness goals, except they will soon gain the ability to dole out rewards accordingly.

Legal work

Smart contracts are already making their way into usage in conjunction with traditional contracts. They make it easier to enact all of the legalese back and forth that is outlined in most contracts when it comes to determining the timing and specifics of certain actions. Smart contracts cut through all this red tape and automate the things that need to happen once certain external factors are met. In theory, if this practice continues to become more common, there will be less a need for this type of boilerplate content in contracts at all as this could all be handled automatically in the blockchain.

Governmental oversight

The federal government has been concerned about the level of anonymity that is provided by the blockchain process for several years since it became apparent that criminals were using bitcoin to launder money, as well as commit various illicit activities.

This leaves cryptocurrency in a bit of a place as the increasing government scrutiny has led to additional levels of checks and balances that were never supposed to be applied to the blockchain in the first place. Furthermore, with the rapidly increasing user base, it will only be a matter of time before it reaches a true saturation point, which will bring about all sorts of issues itself. If these potential issues aren't dealt with before the saturation point is reached, it is unlikely that they ever truly will.

If there is hope for cryptocurrency to eventually become just another part of the incumbent financial system, then it is going to need to find a way to remain true to itself, while also becoming complex enough to meet the needs of everyone who is going to need to use it. It will also need to find a way to be simple enough to use that everyone who is going to want to use it, will be able to.

Clerical tasks

Work is already being done to put smart contracts to work updating and correlating clerical information based on a wide variety of different indicators. They will even have the ability to release specific information after the proper digital signatures have been received. Along these same lines, the technology is poised to revolutionize the shipping industry as supply chain movement of all sorts will soon be clearly visible in a chain that is automatically updated as products move from place to place. Payment will also be handled through the blockchain after the products reach a predetermined location. The same process will handle bills of lading, credit and promise payments.

As the usage rate among manufactures grows, the history of every single product that you receive will grower longer and more detailed until you are able to track the path everything took from the manufacturer straight to your doorstep. Blockchain technology even has the potential to streamline the way voting takes place by allowing for the validation of votes beyond the shadow of a doubt in a process so easy and secure it makes the current voting system look like a travesty.

Conclusion

Ethereum is revolutionizing many aspects of today's digital world. It introduced a new cryptocurrency, the Ether, to rival Bitcoin by not only providing a peer-to-peer medium of exchange but by tying that currency to a particular commodity that people demand: the Ethereum network. Rather than just a currency, Ethereum provides a whole array of Dapps that fundamentally adhere to the philosophies behind the blockchain revolution spawned by Bitcoin. Those philosophies include decentralizing, putting power back into the hands of people, and promoting social justice.

Before you get too involved with Ethereum, you want to know how it's doing. This book explored some of the ways people are using Ethereum, like creating crowd sales, starting autonomous democratic organizations, and building applications. Ethereum is poised to take Bitcoin's place and has grown immensely in very little time. The future is Ethereum is very exciting. Projects focused on prediction markets, identity management, healthcare, and more are all in various phases, and building the foundation of a new internet. The Web 3.0 is going to be decentralized and put power back in the hands of the masses.

Ethereum's future is incredibly bright, not just as a digital currency but as a platform that allows you to run Smart contracts. It is currently helping to accelerate the move from an economy that is well and truly centralized to one that is decentralized, permissionless and borderless, to an economy that is firmly back in the hands of the people.

Decentralized applications have the power and the potential to cause positive disruption to the world, to bring about huge changes to industries like the public sector, health, finance, social media, real estate, insurance, entertainment and much more besides.

With this in mind then, it is clear that you have a choice, find the way in which you can profit from this emergent technology or let the opportunity pass you by and miss out on getting in on the ground floor of the technology that is already being called the most important invention since the internet.

www.ingramcontent.com/pod-product-compliance
Lightning Source LLC
Chambersburg PA
CBHW071219220526
45468CB00002B/674